# **Stepping Up** In Reading

## Phyllis Bertin
## Eileen Perlman

**School Specialty, Inc.**
**Cambridge and Toronto**

**Illustrator:** Elizabeth McGoldrick

Educators Publishing Service

Printed in Benton Harbor, MI, in July 2016
ISBN 978-0-8388-5139-5

13  14  15  16  17  PPG  20  19  18  17  16

# Stepping Up In Reading
## Building Accuracy and Fluency

Reading involves forming a link between speech and print. Students must first learn to decode, that is, to associate the letters with sounds and blend those sounds into words, and then learn to recognize words automatically. Decoding and work recognition are the foundation of reading comprehension. Without these basic skills, children cannot focus on the meaning of text. *Stepping Up In Reading* incorporates all the instructional practices for developing accuracy and fluency in reading that are supported by the latest research. The books contain word, phrase, and sentence lists that provide practice in decoding, word recognition, and expressive reading.

The goal of using these lists is for students to develop the ability to read text so that it sounds like spoken language. The more that oral reading sounds like speech, the better their understanding of the text will be. Therefore, each list should be read and reread with a teacher until students are reading the word lists automatically and reading the phrase and sentence lists with proper expression. The lists are meant to be read under teacher supervision. The teacher should focus students on sound/symbol associations and model blending, proper pronunciation, phrasing, and intonation.

When students are first learning to read, they need reading material in which the vocabulary is controlled to contain only sounds that they have previously learned. Controlled text allows the students to practice their decoding skills and avoid using inappropriate strategies, such as guessing at unfamiliar words. *Stepping Up In Reading 1* contains only short vowels, blends, and common nonphonetic sight words. The *Stepping Up In Reading* books can be used as a supplement to any reading program for developing accurate and fluent reading. The books are, however, one component of the Orton Gillingham-based PAF (Preventing Academic Failure) program, which teaches reading, spelling, and handwriting.

## Word Lists

The word lists contain isolated words without contextual clues, which forces the application of decoding skills. They provide the practice needed to make the transition from deliberate decoding to recognizing words automatically. Words introduced in the word lists are reinforced in the phrase and sentences lists that follow.

Beginning with the first column, have each student take a turn reading one word. If a student does not immediately recognize the word, have him or her decode it by saying the sound of each phonogram and then blending the sounds. Each word must be read as it would naturally be spoken for the student to understand its meaning. Tell the student, *Read it the way you say it.*

## Phrase Lists

The phrase lists allow students to practice reading groups of words in meaningful units, provide examples of proper word usage, and enhance both fluency and comprehension. The practice of reading groups of words is especially important for dysfluent students who read word by word.

Explain to students that the word combinations on the phrase lists are only parts of sentences and therefore lack punctuation. Tell them that the purpose of reading phrases is to practice reading in a way that sounds like the way they speak. Model how phrases should be read until the students read them with the proper intonation.

## Sentence Lists

Sentence lists provide an opportunity to teach students to pay attention to punctuation, such as stopping at periods or pausing at commas, which facilitates reading with expression. The lists also provide practice in reading at an appropriate rate, neither too slowly nor too quickly.

## Activities

Repeated readings of the lists are important to the development of word recognition and fluency. To facilitate the rereading of lists, suggested activities are listed at the bottom of each page. These activities should be done by students as a group under a teacher's guidance. In *Stepping Up In Reading 1* the activities include categorizing, finding synonyms and antonyms, answering the question words, and constructing sentences. The activities ensure that the students are reading for meaning.

All lists should be sent home and read to an adult for extra practice.

**For a full description of the PAF program, visit PAFprogram.com.**

# is

1. Nat is a cat.

2. Nat is fat.

3. Dad is mad.

4. Nat is a fat cat.

5. Nat is sad.

6. Nat is a sad cat.

7. Dan is sad.

8. Dad is a man.

Underline and re-read the sentences that describe how Dan or Dad feels.

# the

1. The cat is fat.

2. Is the man sad?

3. The hat is tan.

4. Can the man nap?

5. Dad had the maps.

6. The cat had a nap on the mat.

7. Is the man mad at the cat?

8. The man had the gas can.

9. Pat the cat.

10. Is the cat fat?

Find and re-read the questions.
Find and re-read the statements.

| | | |
|---|---|---|
| cat | hat | nap |
| sad | am | sat |
| tag | ham | had |
| gas | man | mat |
| fat | map | cap |
| mad | can | pan |
| at | tap | and |

---

| | |
|---|---|
| the fat cat | the tan hat |
| mad at the man | had a map |
| had a nap | a gas can |
| hats and caps | the man and the cats |

Put the phrases into oral sentences.

1. I am mad at the man.

2. Dan had the tan hat.

3. Can Dan tag Sam?

4. Dad had the gas can.

5. Pat the fat cat, Sam.

6. The man had a nap.

7. Is the mat tan?

8. Sam and Dan had ham.

Underline and re-read the sentence with a comma.
Draw a picture to illustrate one of the sentences.

| -at | -an | -ap | -ad | -am |
|-----|-----|-----|-----|-----|
| at | an | tap | dad | am |
| cat | can | cap | sad | ham |
| fat | man | lap | mad | jam |
| mat | fan | map | had | dam |
| pat | pan | sap | pad | |
| sat | tan | | lad | |
| hat | Jan | | | |

| bad | cab | tab |
|-----|-----|-----|
| bat | gab | jab |
| bag | nab | bats |

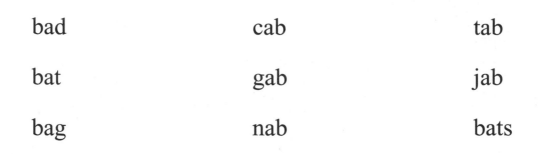

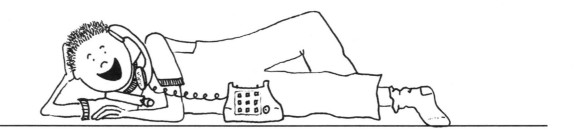

1.  Jan is at bat.

2.  Is Nat a bad cat?

3.  Dan had a tan bag.

4.  The can had a tab.

5.  Nab the bad man!

6.  Can Jan bat?

7.  Jan can gab.

Underline and re-read the sentence with the exclamation point.

| ran | bat | naps |
| rat | jam | cats |
| ram | bag | pats |
| rag | bad | maps |
| rap | and | taps |
| rats | jab | bats |
| raps | had | caps |

1. Dan and Jan ran.

2. Jan had a rag.

3. Nab the rat!

4. Can rats nap?

5. Dad ran and ran.

6. Dan and Jan rap.

Underline and re-read the sentences that are about two people.

**to**

1. Dan ran to Dad.

2. I had to nap.

3. The rat ran to the mat.

4. Dan had to bat.

5. Jan ran to tag Dan.

6. The man had to pat the sad cat.

7. Dad ran to the cab.

Illustrate one of the sentences.

Dad had a tan van.

I had to nap.

Dan is at bat.

The rat ran to the van.

Jan had to pat the sad cat.

The man had caps and bats.

Illustrate each sentence.

| as | rams | lads | tabs |
| has | pans | tags | dads |
| cans | gals | jams | fads |
| vans | fans | hams | dams |
| bags | pads | cabs | rags |

| | |
|---|---|
| 2 cans | 3 bags |
| 3 rags | 2 pans |

Illustrate the phrases in each box.

Dan's cap

Jan's lap

Nat's pan

Sam's van

the cat's mat

Sam's cat

Dad's map

Jan's dad

Dan's bat and cap

the man's hat

1. Dan's cap is tan.

2. The man ran to Sam's van.

3. Jan has Dan's bat and cap.

4. Is the man's hat tan?

5. I am mad at Jan's dad.

6. Pat Dan's cat!

7. The rat ran to the cat's mat.

8. Sam had Nat's pan.

9. Is Nat Sam's cat?

10. Nat is Dan and Jan's cat.

Underline and re-read the sentences that mention a color.

| | | |
|---|---|---|
| **yam** | hat | **yams** |
| **yap** | ham | **yaps** |
| ran | bag | bats |
| as | man | cans |
| van | sad | bags |
| bad | rat | rats |
| jam | rag | rags |
| has | nap | naps |
| had | fan | fans |
| bat | ram | pans |
| dad | tan | maps |
| can | and | hats |

Circle things you can eat.

**you**

1. Can you bat?

2. You can pat Sam's cat.

3. Can you tag Jan?

4. Dan's cat ran to you.

5. Can Dan tag you?

6. Nat ran to you.

Draw a picture to illustrate one of the sentences.

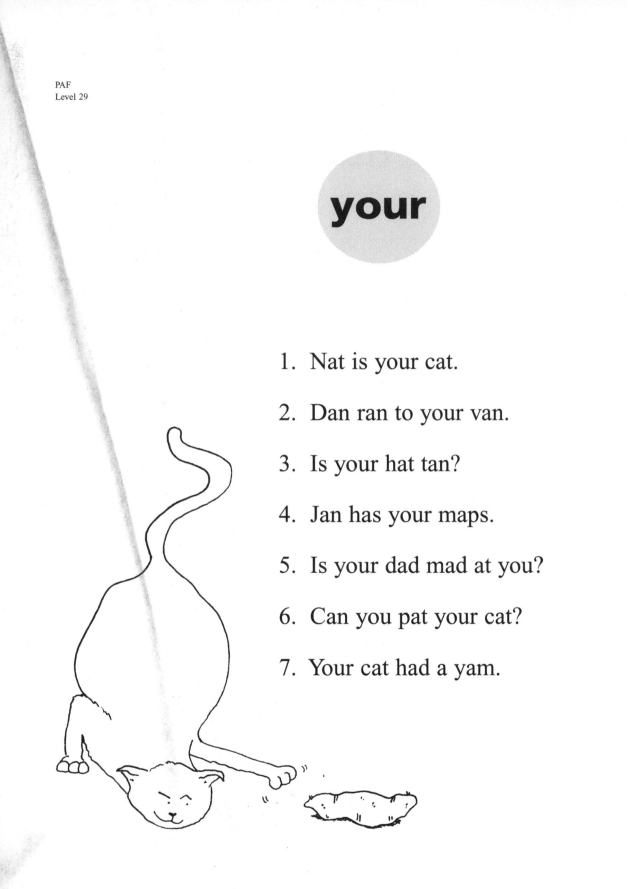

## your

1. Nat is your cat.

2. Dan ran to your van.

3. Is your hat tan?

4. Jan has your maps.

5. Is your dad mad at you?

6. Can you pat your cat?

7. Your cat had a yam.

Circle the phrase in each sentence that shows possession, e.g., *your cat*. Use the phrase in an oral sentence.

| -at | -an | -ap |
|-----|-----|-----|
| at | an | cap |
| cat | can | lap |
| fat | man | nap |
| pat | ran | map |
| sat | fan | tap |
| mat | pan | sap |
| hat | van | |
| bat | Dan | |
| rat | Jan | |

| -ad | -am | -ag |
|-----|-----|-----|
| had | am | bag |
| bad | ham | rag |
| sad | jam | tag |
| mad | dam | gag |
| dad | ram | sag |
| pad | yam | |
| lad | Sam | |

| | |
|---|---|
| had a nap | Rags and Nat |
| Dan's bag | has the jam |
| your tan hat | a tan cap |
| at the mat | your dad's van |
| Sam and Jan | Sam's maps |
| mad at you | at the van |
| the sad man | Nat's pan |
| caps and bats | to the cab |
| the gas can | the bad cat |
| to you | Jan's lap |
| ran and ran | the man and the cats |

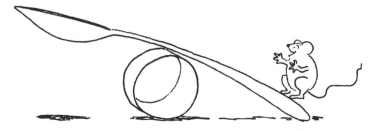

Put the phrases into oral sentences.

16

| ran | bad | hat |
| rat | bat | had |

| pad | dad | can |
| pat | dam | cat |

| man | rap | yam |
| map | rag | yap |

| tag | fat | am |
| tap | fan | at |

| bag | ran | lad |
| bad | ram | lap |

| sat | mad | pal |
| sad | mat | pan |

| naps | taps | raps |
| bats | gabs | sags |
| fans | jabs | nabs |
| pats | nags | lags |
| tags | tans | gags |

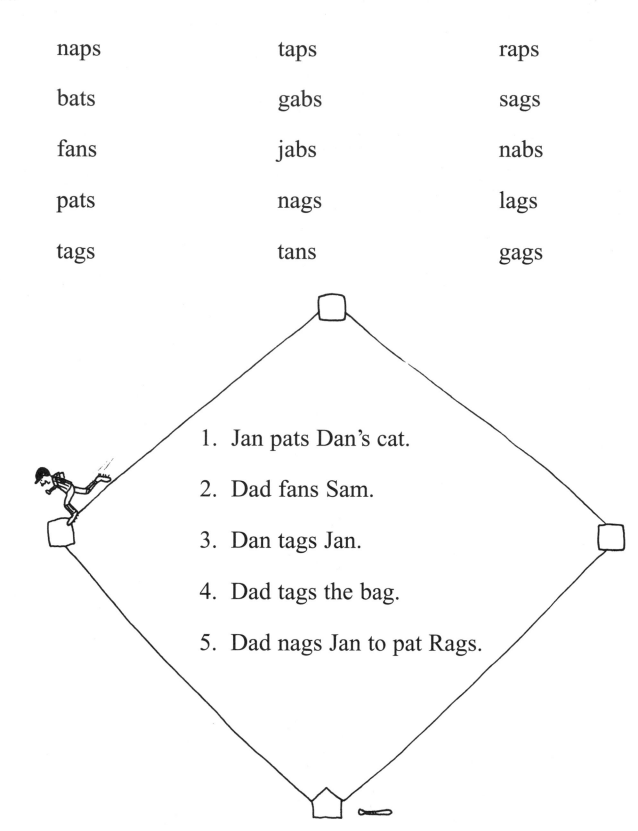

1. Jan pats Dan's cat.

2. Dad fans Sam.

3. Dan tags Jan.

4. Dad tags the bag.

5. Dad nags Jan to pat Rags.

Underline and re-read the sentence that suggests someone may be feeling hot.

| if | hid | nip |
| in | pin | bin |
| it | fit | lip |
| is | pig | rim |
| did | tin | jig |
| his | bit | fin |
| big | pit | fig |
| hit | hip | pigs |
| him | dip | pins |
| sit | lid | sits |
| rip | sip | bits |
| dig | tip | rips |

into

it's

Circle the words that rhyme with *it*.
Underline the words that rhyme with *in*.

| | | |
|---|---|---|
| sat | did | big |
| sit | dad | bag |
| | | |
| is | at | rap |
| as | it | rip |
| | | |
| hit | his | had |
| hat | has | hid |
| | | |
| pan | fit | tin |
| pin | fat | tan |
| | | |
| ham | lap | lid |
| him | lip | lad |
| | | |
| rim | nip | taps |
| ram | nap | tips |
| | | |
| pit | fin | bits |
| pat | fan | bats |

| wag | win | wags | wigs |
|-----|-----|------|------|
| wig | wit | wins | |

---

| | |
|---|---|
| wags and wags | the big pig |
| bats and wins | if I win |
| if it rips | in his van |
| a tin can | into his bag |
| in a bag | as big as a pig |
| if I can | bit into the yam |
| can win | hats and wigs |

Put the phrases into oral sentences.

**said**

1. Dan said, "The bag has a big rip in it."

2. "Nat bit the ham!" said Jan.

3. "I can win," said Sam.

4. Tam said, "Jim's dad has the maps."

5. "It's in the tin can," said Dan's dad.

6. "It fits!" said Jim.

7. Pam said, "I am as big as Dan!"

8. "I hit it and ran," said Sam.

9. "If the bag rips, you can pin it," said Pam's dad.

10. The man said, "The bags fit into the van."

Circle the words that tell who is speaking in each sentence.

ax             six             mix             fax

fix            wax             tax             sax

---

a big ax                      six maps

to fix the van                to mix the wax

six big pigs                  can fax it

had his sax                   can fix it

can wax the van               to mix the dip

Underline and re-read the phrases that describe things you could put in a van. Use these phrases in oral sentences.

1. Is it a big ax

2. Jim had to fix his dad's fan

3. Can six big pigs fit into your van

4. Did Pam mix the dip

5. If the bag rips, I can fix it

6. Is the jam in the big bag

7. Dan bats and wins a pin

8. Can you fax it to Jim

9. Tim bit his lip

10. Did you wax Sid's van

11. It's a bad fit

12. Can you dig a pit and sit in it

Add a period or question mark to each sentence.

24

# of

1.  "Six of the cats ran to Dad," said Jim.

2.  Can you mix the can of wax?

3.  Dad said, "Sid had a bit of jam."

4.  Can you fix the rim of the fan?

5.  Jim said, "The lid fits the rim of the tin can."

6.  Rags had bits of ham in the pan.

7.  Did Jim dip the rag into the can of wax?

8.  Dan has a bag of figs and yams.

Underline and re-read the sentences that name foods.

| hit | if  | did  |
|-----|-----|------|
| him | in  | dig  |
| hid | it  | dip  |

| big | his | rip  |
|-----|-----|------|
| bit | hip | rim  |
| bin | him | rib  |

| is  | fit | pins |
|-----|-----|------|
| it  | fin | pigs |
| if  | fig | pits |

| lip | sit | tin  |
|-----|-----|------|
| lid | sip | tip  |

kit                    kin                    kids

kid                    Kim                    kits

a big kid                  the can of wax

Jim's kit                  a bit of ham

his kin                    in his van

six kits                   had a bad rim

Jim and Kim                in a tin can

ran and hid                the rim of Pam's can

in the bag                 a bad rip

a big pit                  tip of a pad

Sid's wig                  digs and digs

Underline and re-read the phrases that show possession. Use these phrases in oral sentences.

| zip | bad | had |
| zap | hit | pig |
| if | him | fit |
| as | ran | big |
| is | has | win |
| am | can | man |
| in | dig | fix |
| it | sit | pin |
| his | six | and |
| bat | hid | lips |
| mix | bag | zaps |
| did | tin | zips |

Circle things you can hold in your hand.

the can's lid

caps and hats

bits of ham

Jim's map

the fan's rim

big sips

cans of wax

six tin cans

the man's pig

in the bags

a cat's pan

tan vans

Kim's hat

ham and yams

Underline and re-read the phrases that contain words with plural *s*. Use these phrases in oral sentences.

| -in | -it | -ig | -ip | -id | -ix | -im |
|-----|-----|-----|-----|-----|-----|-----|
| in  | it  | big | rip | did | six | him |
| pin | sit | pig | dip | hid | fix | dim |
| tin | fit | dig | lip | rid | mix | rim |
| fin | bit | jig | hip | lid |     |     |
| win | pit | fig | sip | kid |     |     |
| kin | hit | wig | tip |     |     |     |
| bin | kit |     | nip |     |     |     |
|     | wit |     | zip |     |     |     |

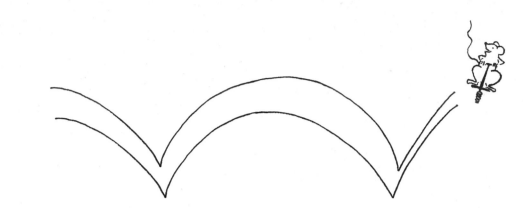

| up | tub | rug |
| us | hug | bun |
| run | cut | mug |
| but | gum | rut |
| fun | dug | jut |
| bus | cub | cubs |
| mud | hut | suds |
| sun | bud | pups |
| bug | tug | buns |
| cup | nut | cups |
| pup | hum | nuts |

Circle the words that rhyme with *cut*.
Underline the words that rhyme with *run*.

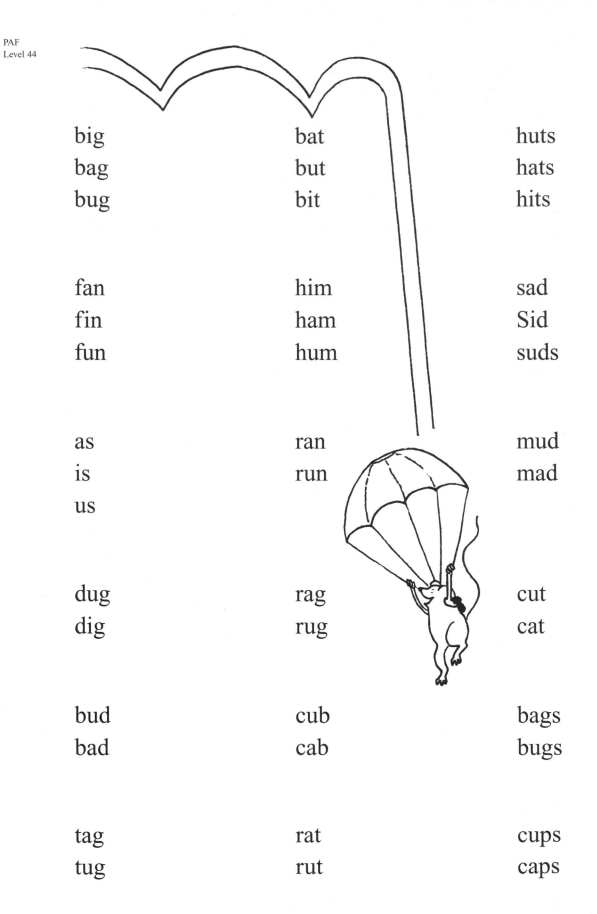

| big | bat | huts |
| bag | but | hats |
| bug | bit | hits |

| fan | him | sad |
| fin | ham | Sid |
| fun | hum | suds |

| as | ran | mud |
| is | run | mad |
| us | | |

| dug | rag | cut |
| dig | rug | cat |

| bud | cub | bags |
| bad | cab | bugs |

| tag | rat | cups |
| tug | rut | caps |

| | |
|---|---|
| in the cup | dug it up |
| rubs and rubs | cut his lip |
| hugs the kids | a tub of suds |
| runs to us | in the bus |
| a tan mug | a big bug |
| as the man runs | a cup of nuts |
| in the mud | runs in the sun |
| hits and runs | zips it up |
| the kid's pup | six big buns |
| bats in a run | run and tag |
| into the sun | into a hut |
| at the bus | six cubs |
| as big as a bus | dug up |
| in a rut | at the big hut |

Underline and re-read the phrases that answer the question *where*. Use these phrases in oral sentences.

have              live              lives

give              gives

1. Give it to us!

2. Did you have fun?

3. "The pigs live in a hut," said Jim.

4. Gus gives the gum to Pam.

5. The buns have nuts.

6. Pam and Jan have pups.

Illustrate one of the sentences.

1. Gus is Pam's dad.

2. Kim said, "Gus runs a big bus."

3. Tam hugs the pups.

4. Is it fun to run in the sun?

5. Bud is Kim's cat.

6. Jan has a bad cut.

7. Gus said to cut up the buns.

8. The ham is big, but it fits in the bag.

9. Is the sun up?

10. Rags runs into the mud.

11. Pam's pup is as big as a pig!

12. Live it up!

Underline and re-read the sentences that discuss animals.

| quiz | wax | pup |
|------|-----|-----|
| quit | us  | mix |
| up   | has | run |
| but  | bag | his |
| six  | fun | cut |
| big  | fix | jam |
| him  | bug | bus |
| mud  | did | rub |
| win  | gum | pig |
| sun  | cup | tub |
| bad  | dug | have |
| hug  | zip | give |

Circle the things that you could put in a bowl.

# are

1. Are you up?

2. The pigs are in the mud.

3. Are you mad at Gus?

4. Jim and Kim are kids.

5. Are Dad and Gus in the big bus?

6. Pam said, "The buns are cut up."

7. Can you have fun if you are sad?

8. The bugs are in the cup!

Illustrate one of the sentences.

| up | tub | mud | sun |
| us | tug | mug | suds |

| but | rug | cup | hug |
| bun | run | cut | hum |
| bud | rub | cub | hut |
| bus | rut | | |
| bug | | | |

1. Are Tam and Dan pals

2. The pups are in Pam's tub

3. Are you as big as Sid

4. Are the mugs yours

5. Jim and Kim are Pam's pals

6. Are his kids big

7. Dan and Jim are pals

Add a period or question mark to each sentence.

1. "They are in the bus," said Gus.

2. Are they in the bag?

3. They have to wax the van.

4. They can run and have fun in the sun.

5. They live in a big hut.

6. Can they hum?

7. They did it!

8. They can run, but can they win?

9. Did they dig a pit?

10. If the bag rips, they can fix it.

11. Kim said, "They are Jim's pals."

12. Are they your cups?

Use the context of the first three sentences to infer who or what *they* might be, *e.g., "They"* in the first sentence might refer to children going to school.

| -un | -ut | -ug | -up | -ub | -us |
|-----|-----|-----|-----|-----|-----|
| run | but | bug | cup | rub | bus |
| fun | cut | hug | pup | tub | Gus |
| sun | hut | dug |     | cub |     |
| bun | nut | rug |     |     |     |
|     | rut | tug |     |     |     |
|     | jut | lug |     |     |     |
|     |     | mug |     |     |     |
|     |     | jug |     |     |     |

| | | |
|---|---|---|
| bug | dig | bad |
| dug | big | dad |

40

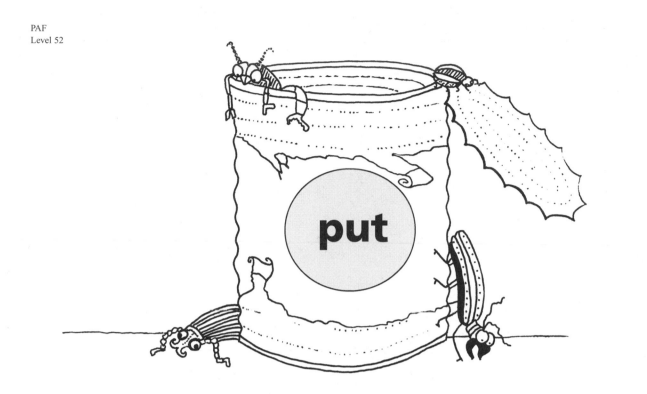

1. The man put his kit into the van.

2. Kim said, "Did you put nuts in the buns?"

3. Put Dan's maps in the bus!

4. Dad puts Rags into the tub.

5. Did Jim put Bud in the sun to sit?

6. "They put the bugs in a tin can," said Dan to Kim.

7. Put the jam into the bag and give it to Gus.

8. Jan puts figs and nuts in the mix.

9. Dan's dad put his mug in the suds.

Underline the words in each sentence that answer the question *where* (e.g., *into the van*).

| | | |
|---|---|---|
| on | hop | jot |
| box | dot | jog |
| not | cot | tot |
| got | ox | pod |
| dog | job | rot |
| pot | log | cob |
| hot | rod | nod |
| fox | sob | dogs |
| mom | hog | tops |
| top | rob | dots |
| mop | mob | mops |

( cannot )

Circle the words that rhyme with *hot*.

| dig | pat | hot |
|-----|-----|-----|
| dug | pot | hat |
| dog | pit | hut |
|     |     | hit |

| top | rib | cap |
|-----|-----|-----|
| tap | rub | cop |
| tip | rob | cup |

| rat | hug | fax |
|-----|-----|-----|
| rut | hag | fix |
| rot | hog | fox |

| cab | not | cots |
|-----|-----|------|
| cub | nut | cats |
| cob | Nat | cuts |

---

| hot | hog | dug |
|-----|-----|-----|
| cot | nut | rub |
| not | dog | hug |
| hut | cut | rob |

43

| on | lot | not |
|----|-----|-----|
| ox | log | nod |

|  | pot | top |
|----|-----|-----|
| dog | pod | tot |
| dot |  |  |

|  | hot | mom |
|----|-----|-----|
| jot | hop | mop |
| job | hog | mob |

| rod | cot | cob |
|-----|-----|-----|
| rot | cod | cop |
| rob | cop | cot |

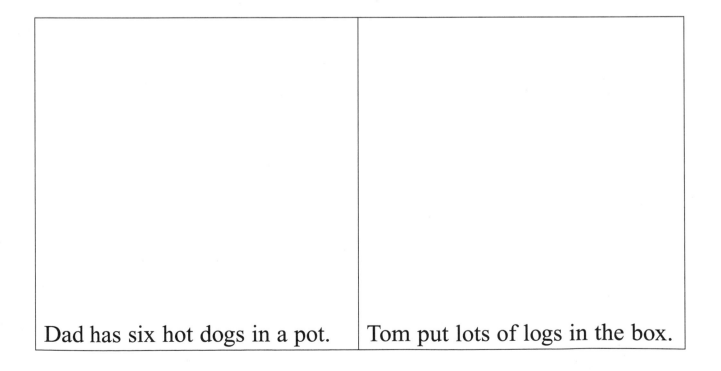

| Dad has six hot dogs in a pot. | Tom put lots of logs in the box. |

Illustrate each sentence.

on the cot

quit his job

lots of pots

pots and pans

hot buns

box tops

a hot pot

hops up

as big as an ox

cannot hop

put it on

the fox cubs

as hot as the sun

Jan's mom

run and jog

the lid of the pot

got rid of

on the log

on top of the box

six fat hogs

a lot of hot suds

pops up

a hot dog on a bun

a big job

Put the phrases into oral questions.

# was

1.  It was hot in the sun!

2.  The lid was on the box.

3.  It was fun to jog and run.

4.  Sam was in the bus, but Gus was not.

5.  Was the ham in the pot?

6.  "Tom was at his job," said Dot.

7.  Dot was sad, but Tom was not.

8.  Mom was not mad at Rags.

9.  Was the hog in the mud hot?

10. The kid was not as big as Jim.

Find the sentences that contain a phrase that answers the question *where* (*e.g.*, in the sun). Underline the phrase and re-read the sentence.

| got | fun | fit |
| ran | tan | wag |
| mom | dot | pot |
| lip | bad | box |
| sad | hop | tip |
| hot | sun | pat |
| tin | not | run |
| sat | pup | hat |
| top | map | dog |

Circle things that are alive.

1. Dot is Dan and Jan's mom

   Is Dot Dan and Jan's mom

2. Is Tom Dan and Jan's dad

   Tom is Dan and Jan's dad

3. The sun was hot

   Was the sun hot

4. Did Tom quit his big job

   Tom quit his big job

5. The ham was in the pot

   Was the ham in the pot

6. Rags is Dan's dog

   Is Rags Dan's dog

7. Did Tom have a nap on the cot

   Tom had a nap on the cot

Add periods and questions marks to the sentences.

| **-ot** | **-og** | **-ob** |
|---------|---------|---------|
| not | dog | job |
| got | log | sob |
| lot | hog | rob |
| pot | jog | mob |
| hot | | cob |
| dot | | |
| cot | | |
| jot | | |
| tot | | |
| rot | | |

| **-od** | **-op** | **-ox** |
|---------|---------|---------|
| rod | top | ox |
| pod | mop | fox |
| cod | hop | box |
| nod | cop | |

| get | met | pep |
| red | yet | bet |
| bed | leg | wed |
| yes | fed | keg |
| let | net | pens |
| men | led | jets |
| wet | den | pets |
| pen | web | hens |
| ten | peg | pegs |
| jet | hem | gets |
| hen | beg | beds |
| pet | vet | legs |

( let's )

Circle the words that rhyme with *get*.

| red | pen | tan | bat |
| rod | pan | ten | bet |
| rid | pin | tin | but |
|     |     |     | bit |

| pat | him | big | bud |
| pet | ham | bag | bad |
| pit | hem | bug | bed |

---

| rid | pin | tin |
| pet | pig | hem |
| red | let | him |
| pit | lid | peg |
| bit | beg | ten |
| lit | pen | bet |
| led | big | wet |

Circle the word in the first column that is a color.
Circle the word in the second column that is something you write with.
Circle the word in the third column that is a number.

| bed | leg | web |
| beg | let | wet |

| yes | bet | hen |
| yet | bed | hem |

| men | pet | beg |
| met | pen | bet |

| peg | web | pet |
| pen | wed | pep |

---

| Ben's red pens | ten men |
| gets him wet | a big bed |
| a wet pet | the red hen |
| a big jet | fed his pet |
| cut his leg | begs and gets fed |
| pens and pads | the pet's vet |

Put the phrases into oral questions.

waxing

boxing

mixing

fixing

taxing

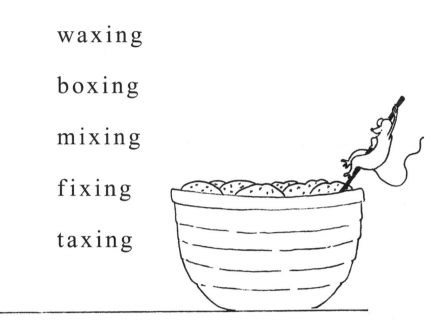

---

fixing the nets

boxing in the den

was mixing jam in the pot

was waxing the van

waxing the red bus

was fixing Ben's bed

are boxing

mixing up the pegs

Draw a line to separate the suffix in each word on the word list.
Read the root word and then the whole word *(wax-waxing)*.
Circle the word with the *doing suffix* in each phrase and sentence.

| not | run | pig |
| --- | --- | --- |
| get | on | yes |
| us | red | lot |
| let | up | sun |
| box | sit | hit |
| wet | men | bed |
| fun | but | has |
| pen | hen | hot |
| bad | ran | and |
| got | dog | ten |
| his | bus | did |
| mom | big | him |

Circle things that might need to be fixed.

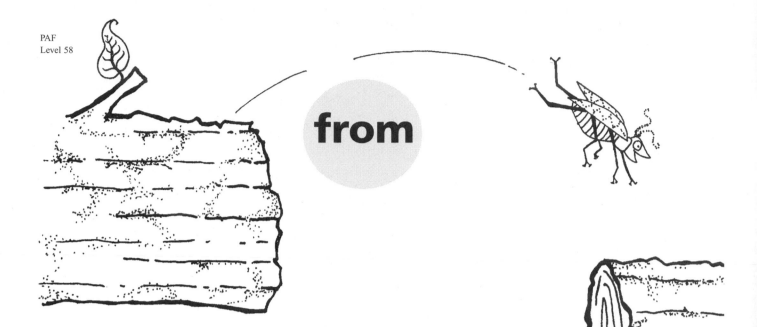

**from**

1. Jim ran from the van to the bus.

2. Get the maps from the van.

3. I got the gum from Ted.

4. "Yes, I got the pets from the vet," said Dot.

5. Are you hot from waxing the bus?

6. The bug can hop from log to log.

7. I am hot from the sun!

8. Jim got a big box from his mom.

9. Did Pam get up from the bed and run to Kim?

10. Kim got pens from Dot, but Jim did not.

Underline and re-read the sentences that tell that someone got something from a person (*e.g., sentence 3*). Circle the words that describe what the person got (*e.g., the gum*).

| -et | -ed | -en | -eg |
|-----|-----|-----|-----|
| get | red | men | leg |
| let | bed | pen | peg |
| wet | led | ten | beg |
| jet | wed | hen | |
| pet | | den | |
| met | | | |
| yet | | | |
| net | | | |
| vet | | | |
| bet | | | |

1.  Ben was fixing the leg of his bed

2.  Rags and Nat are Dan's pets

3.  Are the men on the bus yet

4. "Yes, you can have a pet," said Dot

5.  Did you get the ten pens yet

6.  Ben met Pam at the vet

7.  I can put the wet rag in the tub

Add a period or a question mark to each sentence.

| will | pill | gills |
| tell | sell | tells |
| well | ill | pills |
| fell | sill | bills |
| hill | dull | dolls |
| bell | mill | quills |
| fill | dill | selling |
| doll | quill | yelling |
| bill | bells | telling |
| yell | gull | filling |

Circle the words that are part of an animal.

1. Jim said, "Can you run and yell?"

2. "If I am ill, I will get the pills," said Dot Bell.

3. Is Nat on the sill?

4. Dan Bell fell and hit his leg.

5. Pam was filling the mugs.

6. Dan and Jan Bell ran up the big hill.

7. Ben said, "Will you get it?"

8. Tom Bell was telling Ben to run up the hill.

9. "Tell Dad you fell," said Jan Bell to Dan.

10. Let's fill up the pan and put it on the sill.

11. Tom Bell said, "The man is selling pots and pans."

12. "Get well!" said Dot Bell to Jim.

Underline and re-read the sentences that tell about the Bell family.

| cuff | muff | puffs |
| puff | buff | huffing |
| huff | cuffs | puffing |

---

| huffing and puffing | at the well |
| a quill pen | will get it |
| filling up the gas can | Pam's doll |
| hats and muffs | selling pots and pans |
| on his cuff | had a pill |
| telling him to quit | buffing the van |
| can't yell | gets well |
| yelling at Rags | from hill to hill |
| a dull pin | filling the cup |
| was ill | telling Ben to get in bed |

Underline and reread the phrases that tell what someone might be doing (e.g., *yelling at Rags*).
Decide who might be doing each activity (e.g., *Dad* might be *yelling at Rags*).

| kiss | toss | kissing |
| miss | bass | missing |
| mess | loss | bossing |
| boss | hiss | messing |
| pass | moss | tossing |
| less | lass | passing |
| fuss | mass | hissing |

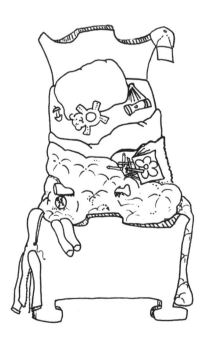

1. Is your bed a mess?

2. Did you kiss your mom?

3. Can a cat hiss at you?

4. Can a van pass a bus?

5. Is a lass a gal?

6. Can a kid have a boss?

7. Can you put a bass in a pan?

Answer each question in a complete oral sentence.

# were

1.  Were Dan and Jan missing Rags?

2.  They were filling up the gas cans.

3.  Were the dolls in the box?

4.  The pigs were in the mud.

5.  Were they yelling at you?

6.  Rags and Nat were messing up Jan's bed.

7. "Were you ill?" said Tom's boss.

8.  Were you and Miss Hill yelling at Rags?

9.  Mom and Dad were kissing the kids.

10.  The cats were hissing at the fox.

11.  The men were fixing the bus.

12.  Miss Hill and I were filling the cups.

Underline and re-read the statements and create a setting for each one (e.g., *They were filling up the gas cans* might take place at a gas station).

| back | dock | ducks |
|------|------|-------|
| sick | wick | socks |
| duck | puck | quacks |
| pack | jack | locks |
| rock | tuck | packs |
| luck | sack | tacks |
| lick | buck | quacking |
| lock | nick | pecking |
| sock | lack | tacking |
| pick | rack | kicking |
| kick | peck | picking |
| deck | quack | locking |
| tack | quick | licking |
| neck | rocks | packing |

Circle all the words that rhyme with *back*.

packing the bag

a sick dog

ten ducks

picking up the tacks

a big sack of jacks

red and tan socks

had bad luck

locking the van

a pack of gum

will run and kick

on the sun deck

in his backpack

tucking it in

backing up

a tan sack

will put it back

a big rock

on his neck

as quick as a fox

tick-tock

a pack of dogs

picking up the mess

Underline and re-read the phrases that tell what someone is doing now.

63

| add | fuzz | eggs |
| odd | buzz | mitts |
| egg | jazz | adding |
| mitt | fizz | buzzing |
| mutt | adds | fizzing |

1. The ham and eggs were fizzing in the pan.

2. "Add six and ten," said Dot to Jan.

3. The odd man put rocks into his backpack.

4. Ben put his bats and mitts into the van.

5. "Tom is adding up the bill," said Kim.

6. Kim said, "Is Rags a mutt?"

7. Were the bugs buzzing on the sun deck?

8. Jim's dad said, "Jazz is fun!"

Underline and re-read the sentences that quote someone. Circle the speakers in these sentences.

| sell | hill | eggs |
| kiss | add | bells |
| back | sick | adds |
| will | miss | socks |
| luck | lick | packing |
| pass | tell | huffing |
| rock | duck | puffing |
| fell | puff | adding |
| odd | lock | kissing |
| less | mess | telling |

Circle things that can be found in a home.

1. Dot said, "Pack your bag and put it on the bed."

2. The duck sat on the rock and said, "Quack! Quack!"

3. Tim's sick dog is at the vet.

4. "Quick! Put Pam's doll back," said Gus to Kim.

5. Did you have bad luck?

6. "Pick up your socks!" yells Kim.

7. "Lock the bats and mitts in Sam's van," said Ben.

8. Kim ran from rock to rock and fell into the mud.

Underline and re-read the sentences in which someone is being told to do something.

| | | | |
|---|---|---|---|
| mixed | licked | kicked | quacked |
| waxed | fixed | locked | messed |
| packed | picked | passed | ticked |
| kissed | missed | tossed | pecked |

---

packed his bag

quacked and quacked

passed the buns

mixed up

waxed and buffed

kissed mom

picked up the mess

fixed the bells

kicked and missed

tossed it back

missed the kids

locked the van

messed up

pecked at the bugs

Draw a line to separate the suffix in each word on the word list.
Read the root word and then the whole word (*mix-mixed*).
Have each student choose a word and use it in an oral sentence.

# very

1. Kim was very mad at Tim.

2. Is your pet very sick?

3. Jan said, "Nat is a very bad cat."

4. Was Ben very sick?

5. He is not very ill.

6. Tim's socks got very wet in the mud.

7. Are the pins very dull?

8. Dan picked up a very big rock and put it in the van.

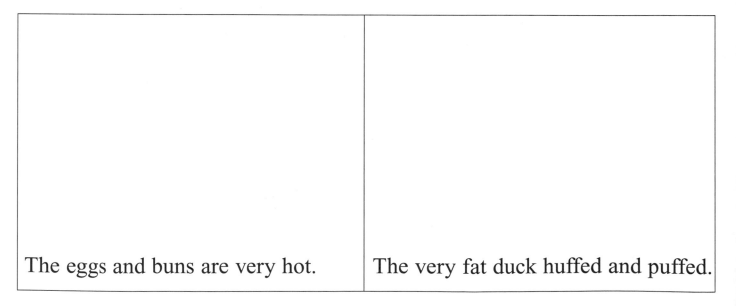

| The eggs and buns are very hot. | The very fat duck huffed and puffed. |

Illustrate the sentences.

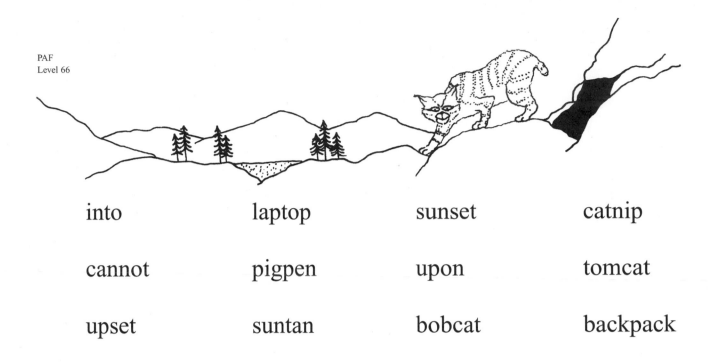

into        laptop        sunset        catnip

cannot        pigpen        upon        tomcat

upset        suntan        bobcat        backpack

1. They sat on the deck at sunset.

2. Ben fixed his pigpen.

3. Put your pens and laptop in your backpack.

4. Kim gives Bud a bit of catnip.

5. Bobcats live in dens.

6. Ben cannot add well.

7. Did the mess upset Dot?

8. The tomcat fell into the pit.

Divide each compound word on the list into its component words, e.g., *in/to*.
Circle the compound words in each sentence.
Underline and re-read the sentence with two compound words.

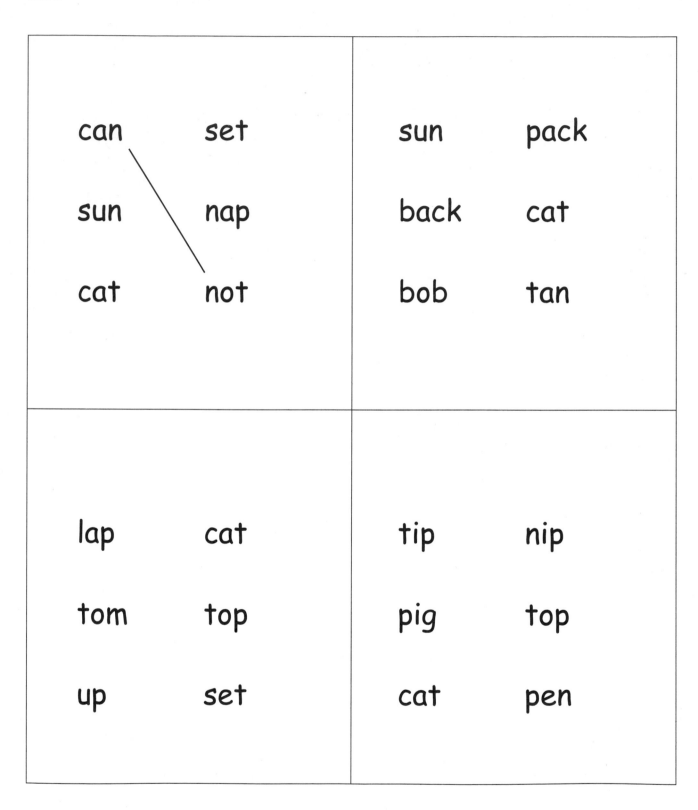

| | | | |
|---|---|---|---|
| can | set | sun | pack |
| sun | nap | back | cat |
| cat | not | bob | tan |
| lap | cat | tip | nip |
| tom | top | pig | top |
| up | set | cat | pen |

Draw a line from a word in the first column to a word in the second column to create a compound word. Read the compound words.

| this | that | math |
|------|------|------|
| then | with | thin |
| path | bath | thick |
| them | thud | bathtub |

that's

---

| a thick pad | with you |
|-------------|----------|
| this backpack | in the bathtub |
| on the path | gives it to them |
| with his boss | a math quiz |
| thin legs | with a kiss |
| had a bath | waxed that hot rod |
| this and that | then kissed his mom |

Underline and re-read the phrases that tell *where*.

**do**

1. Do your math and then put it in your backpack.

2. Give them this to do!

3. Do not run on the path.

4. I am fixing the bed and then I can do that with you.

5. Gus said, "Do not sit on top of the van!"

6. "I can do math with you," said Jim.

7. Do you miss them?

8. Did you do that math with your dad?

9. Do not yell at that very sick dog!

10. Kim and Pam are doing a jig.

11. Do not put the rocks into that backpack.

12. "I am not doing the pots, but you can do them!"
    said Dot.

Underline and re-read the sentences that are commands.

| | |
|---|---|
| me | me |
| | men |
| he | he |
| | hen |
| go | go |
| | got |
| we | we |
| | wet |
| no | no |
| | not |
| so | so |
| | sob |
| be | be |
| | beg |
| yo-yo | |
| going | |
| being | |

1. Can he run up the path?

2. Give the eggs to me.

3. Dan is sick so he cannot jog with me.

4. He packed the box with eggs.

5. We have to tell Dad to fix this lock.

6. "Do not be so sad," said Dan's mom.

7. The vet said, "We have no pills to give that sick dog."

8. Tell me if you are going with us.

9. He has a red yo-yo in his backpack.

10. We are so upset that you missed going with us.

11. Go get into the bathtub!

12. "Jim is being bad, so he is not going with us," said Dot to Tom.

13. Rags fell in the mud so he will have to have a bath.

14. "That's so sad!" said Kim's mom to Miss Hill.

Underline and re-read the sentences in which someone is quoted.
Circle the word or words that tell who is speaking.

1. Dad said that this rag goes in the bathtub.

2. This pen goes with that pad.

3. Ben goes into the van with Dad.

4. Mom said that I can go if Dad goes.

5. Rags goes with Nat to the pigpen.

6. This bad egg goes back in the box.

7. Tim goes to math with Jan.

8. Dad goes to his job in a cab.

9. The jet goes fast.

10. Dan goes to bed at ten.

Underline the words in each sentence that tell what or who *goes* (e.g., *this rag* in the first sentence).

| much | chat | chicks |
|------|------|--------|
| chop | chick | chats |
| chin | chum | chills |
| such | check | chops |
| rich | chess | chips |
| chip | chill | checked |

| inch | pinch | punched |
|------|-------|---------|
| lunch | bunch | pinching |
| ranch | quench | pinched |
| punch | hunch | munched |
| bench | munch | lunchbox |

Circle the words with the past-time suffix.

1. Mr. Tom Bell is Jan and Dan's dad.

2. Mr. Bell checked Jan's math.

3. "I can chip the logs with your ax," said Mr. Mills.

4. Mr. Mills is such a rich man that he has a big ranch.

5. The hen was in the pen with the chicks.

6. Mr. Mills had a chat with his chum, Mr. Bell.

7. Kim said, "Mom put a can of punch in my lunchbox."

8. Mr. Bell sat on a bench and munched chips.

9. "I have so much math to do," said Pam.

10. Gus said, "If you do your math, then you can go to Mr. Mack's ranch."

Underline and re-read the sentences that tell about Dan and Jan's father.

| itch | latch | pitching |
|------|-------|----------|
| catch | hitch | matching |
| pitch | hutch | hatched |
| match | batch | pitched |
| ditch | fetch | catching |
| hatch | notch | hatching |
| witch | itched | patched |
| patch | itching | matchbox |

---

had an itch

pitch and catch

a matched set

into the ditch

to put a patch on

hatched from eggs

the witch's hat

a batch of nuts

Dot's matchbox

can run and fetch

Put the phrases into oral sentences.

| going | pitching | checked |
| chops | doing | punched |
| hatching | chills | munched |
| being | pinched | pigpens |
| catching | chips | pitched |
| checking | hatched | matching |
| chicks | pinching | pecked |
| patched | kissed | laptops |
| quacking | locked | missing |
| patching | kicking | backpacks |

Draw a line to separate the suffix in each word on the word list.
Read the root word and then the whole word (*go-going*).
Have each student choose a word and use it in an oral sentence.

my laptop

my mom and dad

by the bench

in my lunchbox

my very rich pal

by the bed

my boss

by the ditch

with my chums

by the pigpen

my red yo-yo

in my backpack

by the rocks

my bat and mitt

by the bathtub

on my chin

going to my ranch

by the dock

Underline and re-read the phrases that answer the question *where*.

| this | check | than |
| much | that | rich |
| lunch | itch | catch |
| math | such | chip |
| chop | ranch | then |
| into | with | path |
| hatch | bunch | thin |
| them | inch | cannot |
| witch | match | chin |
| thick | bath | chick |

Find a word in the first column that is the opposite of *thin*.
Find a word in the second column that is a unit of measurement.
Find a word in the third column that is a part of the body.

1. If Jet gets sick, Dr. Mack will give him pills.

2. Do not put rocks in my backpack!

3. My dad can't pitch but my mom can.

4. "I am a vet," said Dr. Mack.

5. Pick the chips up and put them in my lunchbox.

6. "Is Dr. Mack your vet?" said Dot.

7. Dr. Mack sat by the rocks and had lunch.

8. Dot said, "Quick! Put that back in the box."

9. Dr. Mack is a vet on TV.

10. Did your chicks hatch yet?

11. Do not yell at me!

12. Dr. Mack said, "If my van has no gas, then it cannot go."

Underline and re-read the sentences about Dr. Mack.

| | | |
|---|---|---|
| she | dash | shell |
| wish | shot | shock |
| fish | ash | shack |
| ship | shed | shellfish |
| shut | shin | wished |
| dish | gash | rushing |
| rush | cash | shells |
| shop | shy | wishing |
| rash | mash | rushed |
| hush | lash | shocking |

Circle the word in the first column that means the same as *store*.
Circle the word in the second column that is a kind of money.
Circle the word in the third column that means the same as *shed*.

83

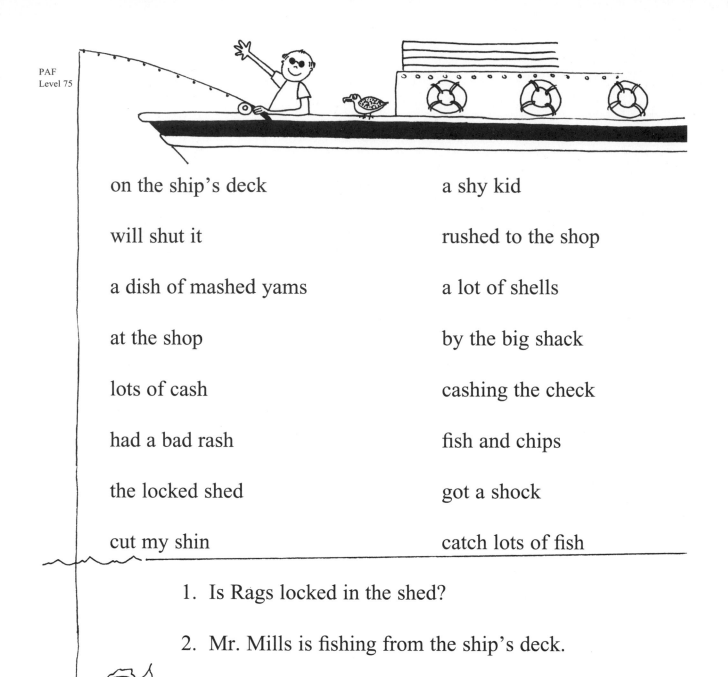

| on the ship's deck | a shy kid |
| will shut it | rushed to the shop |
| a dish of mashed yams | a lot of shells |
| at the shop | by the big shack |
| lots of cash | cashing the check |
| had a bad rash | fish and chips |
| the locked shed | got a shock |
| cut my shin | catch lots of fish |

1. Is Rags locked in the shed?

2. Mr. Mills is fishing from the ship's deck.

3. The mashed yams are hot, but the dish is not.

4. I wish I were rich.

5. Dr. Mack fixed the rash on Nat's leg.

6. If Dan gets the fan wet, he will get a bad shock.

7. Ben said, "Put the fish and chips in my dish."

Underline and re-read the phrases that are about money.

| isn't | he's | you're |
|---|---|---|
| didn't | she's | we're |
| wasn't | it's | I'll |
| hasn't | that's | he'll |
| aren't | I'm | she'll |
| haven't | let's | we'll |

1. That's not my backpack!

2. Kim isn't shy, but Jim is.

3. I'll pack your lunchbox.

4. Dan didn't go fishing with his dad.

5. The chicks haven't hatched yet.

6. We're not going with you to the ranch.

7. She'll put the can of punch in your lunchbox.

8. Let's go!

9. He's a very thin man.

10. "You're my pal," said Dan to Kim.

Re-read the list of contractions, saying the two words that each contraction represents.
Underline the contraction in each sentence and re-read the sentence substituting the two words
that each contraction represents.

| ship | chip | cashing |
| mash | hatch | mashed |
| hutch | ditch | catching |
| witch | chin | wishing |
| catch | wish | matched |
| chop | match | cashed |
| cash | dish | wished |
| hush | shin | mashing |
| hash | shop | hatched |

Re-read the last column, saying each word and then the root word (e.g., *cashing - cash*).

don't

1.  Don't run with that dish!

2.  Gus said, "Don't do that!"

3.  If they don't lock the shed, we can put the pick and ax back.

4.  We'll go get the fish, if you don't go.

5.  Don't be in such a rush!

6.  I don't have my lunchbox with me.

7.  "We don't sell chess sets in this shop," said Mr. Mills.

8.  If you are sick, then don't kiss me!

9.  Don't yell at me if you're upset!

10.  Don't put that bunch of rags in the back of my van.

Underline and re-read the sentences in which someone is being told not to do something that could be dangerous.

# won't

1. Mr. Bell won't go to the shop with me.

2. The dish won't fit on the rack.

3. Tom said to Gus, " I won't go fishing with you."

4. Won't you miss us if we go?

5. If you won't do your math, then you can't go with us.

6. Won't you get hot if you sit in the sun?

7. "I won't catch, but I'll pitch," said Ben.

8. "I won't let you go to the ranch," said Mr. Bell.

9. Jim won't put the chess set back in the box.

Underline and re-read the sentence about baseball.

88

| | |
|---|---|
| bang | long |
| sang | gong |
| hang | song |
| gang | tongs |
| rang | songs |
| pang | banging |
| fangs | hanging |

---

| | |
|---|---|
| banging the pans | hums a song |
| hangs the rag up | hangs on |
| sang the songs | a long nap |
| rang the bell | bangs the gong |
| its long fangs | not very long |

Put the phrases into oral sentences.

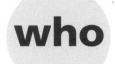

# who

1. Who rang the bell?

2. If I get sick, who will give me my pills?

3. Who sang the song?

4. Who is banging the pans?

5. Who is in the gang?

6. If I get the dolls, who will sell them?

7. Tell me who put the shellfish in my dish.

8. Who is banging on the rock?

9. Mr. Bell said, "Who is it?"

10. I'll tell you who is going with us.

Underline and re-read the sentence in which someone might be eating.

king                    thing                    singing

sing                    rings                    ringing

ring                    wings                    ping-pong

wing                    sings                    ding-dong

---

1. Who put that thing in my dish?

2. The king is singing in his bathtub.

3. Mr. Bell will pack the ring in the box and give it to Dot.

4. Do fish have wings?

5. I'll sing a song for you.

6. The bells are ringing.

7. Ducks have wings and can fly.

8. Will my things fit in your backpack?

9. The cat's bell goes ding-dong as it runs.

Underline and re-read the sentence in which someone will get a gift.

| hung | sung | rungs | lungs |
|------|------|-------|-------|
| bang | ring | rang | ping-pong |
| king | wing | hung | ding-dong |
| gong | sang | rings | hanging |
| hang | gang | rungs | singing |
| long | sung | fangs | banging |

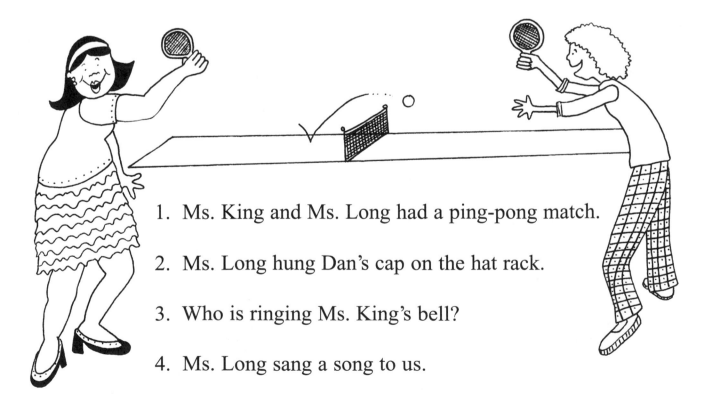

1. Ms. King and Ms. Long had a ping-pong match.

2. Ms. Long hung Dan's cap on the hat rack.

3. Who is ringing Ms. King's bell?

4. Ms. Long sang a song to us.

Circle the words that are part of an animal.

1. "The school bell has rung," said Ms. King.

2. Dan rushed to catch the school bus.

3. Ms. Long said, "We sing songs in school."

4. Kim goes to school with Jim.

5. Mom picked up the kids at school.

6. "We have to get things for school," said Tam's mom.

7. Is that your school?

8. "Do you have your lunchbox in school with you?"
   said Mr. Mills.

9. Is that a school of fish going by the ship?

Underline and re-read the sentence that describes something that happened after school.

# VC/CV

| | | |
|---|---|---|
| rabbit | happen | napkin |
| picnic | basket | until |
| rocket | button | jacket |
| lesson | magnet | bottom |
| kitten | tennis | ticket |
| ribbon | channel | suffix |
| tunnel | bucket | sudden |
| attic | funnel | goblin |
| muffin | gallon | helmet |
| puppet | public | pocket |

Circle the word in the first column that is part of a house.
Circle the word in the second column that is a sport.
94 Circle the words in the third column that can be worn.

the rabbit's den

a tennis racket

in the picnic basket

the rocket ship

six buttons

his hat and jacket

top and bottom

into the funnel

did not happen

the math lesson

picks up the tickets

up in the attic

his back pocket

a school picnic

his red helmet

hot muffins

into the tunnel

channel ten

a velvet ribbon

a sudden chill

adding a suffix

a gallon of milk

a muffin mix

a shy kitten

public school

very common

not until lunch

a witch and a goblin

Underline and re-read the phrases which describe things that someone can wear.

95

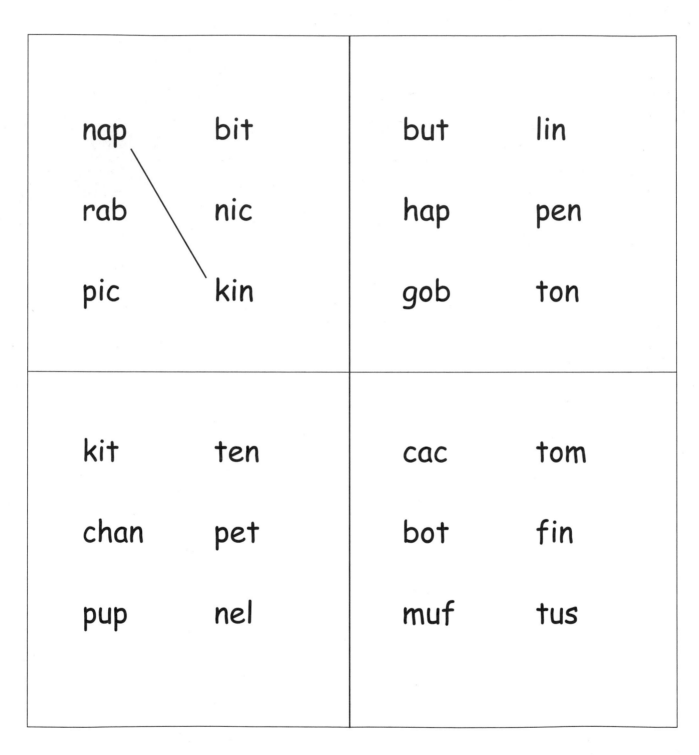

| | | | |
|---|---|---|---|
| nap | bit | but | lin |
| rab | nic | hap | pen |
| pic | kin | gob | ton |
| kit | ten | cac | tom |
| chan | pet | bot | fin |
| pup | nel | muf | tus |

Draw a line from a syllable in the first column to a syllable in the second column to create a word.
Read the words.

| axes | benches | dishes |
| taxes | lunches | kisses |
| boxes | ranches | ditches |
| wishes | bunches | bosses |
| inches | lashes | rashes |
| witches | matches | lunchboxes |

boxes of dishes                    sat on the benches

ten inches                         packed the lunches

bunches of ribbons                 a box of matches

a set of dishes                    six inches of ribbon

dug the ditches                    lots of kisses

the kids' lunchboxes               witches and goblins

Draw a line to separate the suffix in each word on the word list.
Read the root word and then the whole word (*ax-axes*).
Underline and re-read the phrases that tell what someone did.

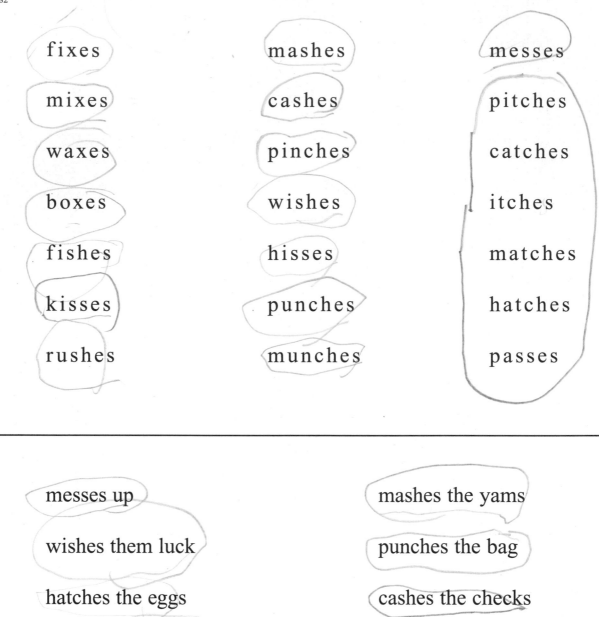

fixes

mixes

waxes

boxes

fishes

kisses

rushes

mashes

cashes

pinches

wishes

hisses

punches

munches

messes

pitches

catches

itches

matches

hatches

passes

messes up

wishes them luck

hatches the eggs

munches on chips

rushes to school

mashes the yams

punches the bag

cashes the checks

passes the dishes

hisses at the rabbits

Draw a line to separate the suffix in each word on the word list. Read the root word and then the whole word (*fix-fixes*). Put the phrases into oral sentences.

elf

self

shelf

gulf

golf

golfing

myself

himself

yourself

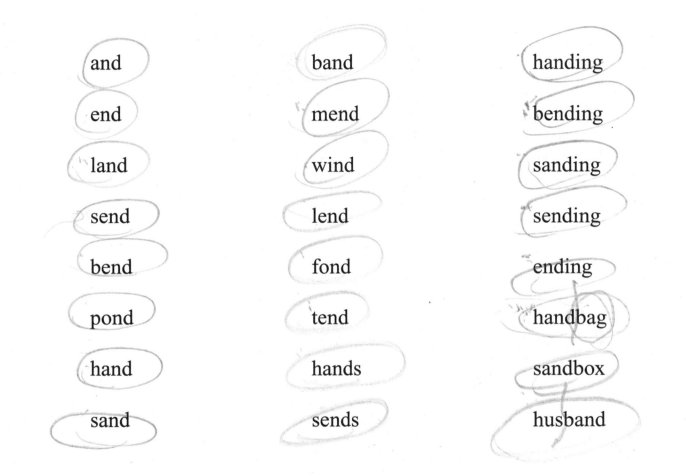

and

end

land

send

bend

pond

hand

sand

band

mend

wind

lend

fond

tend

hands

sends

handing

bending

sanding

sending

ending

handbag

sandbox

husband

Circle things that are found outdoors.

1. Mrs. Sands said, "Will you lend me your tennis racket?"

2. Mr. and Mrs. Benton are golfing.

3. Mr. Sands hung up the shelf by himself.

4. Miss Hill put the boxes of muffin mix on the top shelf.

5. Ms. Mills said, "Who is in the school band?"

6. Mr. Bell put the kid's bucket in the sandbox.

7. "I'll mend the socks by myself," said Mrs. Bell.

8. Hand in your lessons to Ms. King.

9. Mrs. Benton's husband is sanding the picnic benches.

10. "Put the picks and axes in the shed yourself," yells Mrs. Benton.

Underline and re-read the sentences that talk about men.

| | | |
|---|---|---|
| magnet | tablet | atlas |
| until | cotton | socket |
| happen | gossip | index |
| basket | gallon | festive |
| button | mascot | common |
| cactus | publish | pastel |
| channel | ticket | locket |
| lesson | muffin | fossil |
| rocket | attic | funnel |
| ribbon | gallop | tonsils |
| jacket | pocket | cutlet |
| puppet | public | velvet |
| rabbit | napkin | suffix |
| sudden | kitten | album |
| goblin | bottom | bandit |

Circle two things in the first column that can grow.
Circle three things in the second column that are made of paper.
Circle two words in the third column that are types of books.

101

| | | |
|---|---|---|
| ant | vent | panting |
| went | bent | hinting |
| pant | lint | renting |
| pants | lent | hunting |
| tent | tint | denting |
| hint | ants | chanting |
| rent | runt | absent |
| sent | chant | invent |
| hunt | mints | consent |
| dent | rents | distant |
| mint | hunts | inventing |

Circle the word in the first column that is the opposite of *stayed*.
Circle the word in the second column that means the opposite of *straight*.
Circle the word in the third column that means the opposite of *near*.

| | |
|---|---|
| absent from school | went hunting |
| dents Sid's van | an ant hill |
| put up his tent | sent up a rocket |
| gives me a hint | will mend the pants |
| attic vents | boxes of mints |
| bent his legs | chanting the song |
| a panting dog | lent him my tennis racket |
| rents a big van | bent in the wind |
| lent mom a hand | my husband's pants |

Underline and re-read the phrase in the first column that tells that someone was helpful.
Underline and re-read the phrase in the second column that tells that someone will be helpful.
Use these phrases in oral sentences.

| | |
|---|---|
| singer | sander |
| boxer | rancher |
| mixer | pitcher |
| locker | punter |
| hunter | lender |
| seller | sender |
| golfer | catcher |
| packer | passer |
| renter | rocker |

Draw a line to separate the suffix in each word on the word list.
Read the root word and then the whole word (*sing-singer*).
Circle the words that have to do with sports.

1. If the hunter catches a fox, will he let it go?

2. The fisherman pitched his tent by the pond.

3. Mrs. Benton said, "We can't have muffins until Tom fixes my mixer."

4. Jim put his catcher's mitt in the locker.

5. They yelled at the punter, "Kick it! Kick it!"

6. The teller cashed Mr. Bell's check.

7. The boxers went into the ring.

8. Who is the singer in your band?

9. "I'll fix your rocker," said Mr. Benton, "but I'll have to rent a sander."

10. The packers put the boxes in the back of Sam's van.

Circle the doer suffix words that refer to things (e.g., *rocker*) rather than people (e.g., *hunter*).

| -ank | -ink | -unk |
|------|------|------|
| bank | ink | junk |
| sank | pink | sunk |
| thank | wink | chunk |
| yank | think | dunk |
| hank | sink | bunk |
| rank | link | hunk |
| tank | rink | |
| thanks | mink | |
| banker | thinking | |

thanks a lot

winked at me

thinking of you

thank you

a pink cotton jacket

the singer's husband

bunk beds

a big tank of fish

the junk shop

yanked the fishing rod

the catcher and the pitcher

red ink

sank to the bottom

ten hunters

filling up the gas tank

the dishes in the sink

a big boxer

a teller at the bank

went to the bank

dunks it in the basket

a school of fish

a set of dishes

as quick as a wink

a chunk of ham

sinking in the pond

a rich banker

Underline and re-read the phrases that tell *who*. Put these phrases into oral sentences.

| fast | rest | cast |
| just | fist | mast |
| best | vest | quest |
| must | cost | nests |
| test | bust | dusting |
| rust | past | listing |
| west | chest | resting |
| pest | last | testing |
| mist | dust | dustpan |
| lost | gust | contest |
| list | nest | dentist |

Circle the word in the first column that is a direction.
Circle the word in the second column that is a piece of furniture.
**108** Circle the word in the third column that is an occupation.

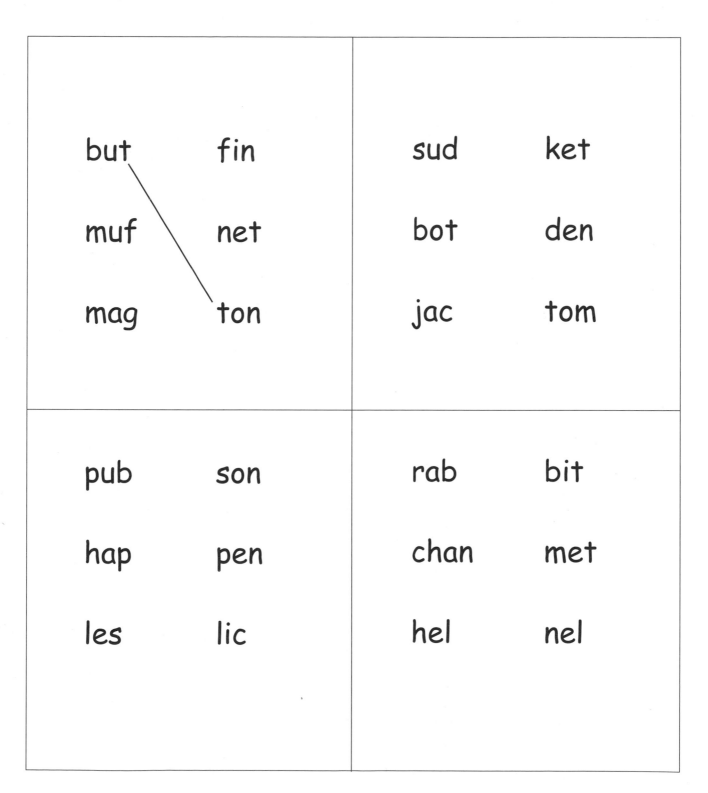

but        fin

muf        net

mag        ton

sud        ket

bot        den

jac        tom

pub        son

hap        pen

les        lic

rab        bit

chan       met

hel        nel

Draw a line from a syllable in the first column to a syllable in the second column to create a word. Read the words.

| faster | duller | sicker |
|--------|--------|--------|
| richer | longer | fonder |
| quicker | thicker | pinker |

1.  Dan can't run faster than his dad.

2.  Is Ben richer than Gus Sands?

3.  I have to put up a shelf that is ten inches longer than this.

4.  Pam ran up the hill quicker than Tam did.

5.  Is mud thicker than milk?

6.  Tom is fonder of chess than checkers.

7. "You will get sicker if you don't get in bed to rest," said
   Dr. Nick to Kim.

8.  My jacket is thick, but yours is thicker.

Underline and re-read the sentence that is a warning.

| | Suffix Means More | The Doer Suffix |
|---|---|---|
| fast(er | X | |
| singer | | |
| hunter | | |
| quicker | | |
| catcher | | |
| richer | | |
| seller | | |
| longer | | |
| duller | | |
| packer | | |
| thinker | | |
| pitcher | | |
| sicker | | |

Take the suffix off each word. Decide whether the suffix means *more* or the *doer* and put an X in the appropriate column.

| ask | husk | left | loft |
| mask | disk | lift | soft |
| desk | task | gift | shift |
| tusk | dusk | raft | lifting |
| risk | asked | sift | softer |

1. Mrs. Bell asked her husband to lift the chest for her.

2. Did you put the disks on my desk?

3. Mr. and Mrs. Benton went rafting with the kids.

4. I think kittens are softer than dogs.

5. Dan asked his mom to get him a mask.

6. Kim left the rest of the gifts in Ben's van.

7. Jim bats with his left hand.

Underline and re-read the sentence that expresses an opinion.

112

| gifts | messes | tells |
| cashes | inches | lunches |
| kisses | lifts | itches |
| tests | dishes | tacks |
| boxes | catches | desks |
| asks | thinks | rushes |
| baths | hands | songs |
| wishes | masks | pitches |
| lists | hatches | buzzes |
| matches | fixes | misses |
| lands | tents | waxes |

---

| hatches eggs | cashes the checks |
| gifts in boxes | pitches the tents |
| lots of kisses | lifts up his hands |
| pitches and catches | lists of wishes |
| waxes the desks | misses the bus |

Draw a line to separate the suffix in each word on the word list. Read the root word and then the whole word (*gift-gifts*).

| | | | |
|---|---|---|---|
| her | chapter | summer | rubber |
| after | silver | better | litter |
| sister | shelter | dinner | hammer |
| under | tender | letter | otter |
| number | lumber | butter | supper |
| ladder | temper | timber | bitter |
| winter | master | pepper | offer |
| thunder | enter | banner | jitters |

Circle the words that are things a builder might use.

114

| | |
|---|---|
| a long chapter | my sister |
| last summer | ran after her |
| bus shelter | muffin batter |
| a hammer and an ax | lost his temper |
| enters the school | a winter jacket |
| the dog's master | bitter pills |
| a rubber duck | on the rungs of the ladder |
| a litter of kittens | after supper |
| after dinner | her silver ring |
| an odd number | six letters |
| a job offer | under the desk |
| hot red pepper | picking up the litter |

Underline and re-read the phrases in the first column that tell *when*.
Underline and re-read the phrases in the second column that tell *where*.
Put these phrases into oral sentences.

| lifted | landed | dusted | listed |
|--------|--------|--------|--------|
| hunted | rested | lasted | mended |
| rusted | handed | hinted | dented |
| added | ended | rented | tended |

---

lifted her hands

landed in the pond

rested on her bunk bed

ended the letter

lasted until the winter

mended her socks

a rusted hammer

added up the numbers

handed me the pepper mill

dusted under the desk

rented a van

dented the fender

Have each student choose a word and use it in an oral sentence.
Underline and re-read the phrases that tell what someone could have done at home.

**want**

1. If you want help, just ask for it.

2. This summer, we want to go rafting with the Bentons.

3. Ben wants a nap after lunch so he will be rested.

4. My sister wants me to send the letters that are on the desk.

5. We'll ask Kim if she wants to go to school with us.

6. Mrs. Bell wants to give a silver ring to her husband.

7. Who wants to go fishing after supper?

8. I wanted butter for the hot muffins.

9. Dad wanted us to dust under the beds.

10. Dad wants a hammer so he can fix the rung of the ladder.

11. Dan thinks he wants to be a singer.

12. Do you want to give your sister a hand with the dinner dishes?

Underline and re-read the two sentences that tell *why* someone wants something.

| lost | thank | under |
| hand | desk | after |
| went | land | happen |
| bank | pink | enter |
| fast | best | winter |
| west | wind | until |
| ask | think | sister |
| her | left | better |
| must | send | lesson |
| last | list | chapter |
| sent | past | number |
| rest | himself | bottom |
| end | myself | summer |
| test | yourself | letter |
| just | herself | sudden |

Circle the things that can be found in school.

belt              kilt              elk

quilt             milk             melt

silk              tilt              quilted

felt              melting          milking

tilted the ladder          the quilted jacket

a soft pink quilt          a cup of milk

melted butter             is melting

as soft as silk           hunted the elks

a silk belt               felt wet

felt better               men in kilts

Underline and re-read the phrases that describe things made of material. Use these phrases in oral sentences.

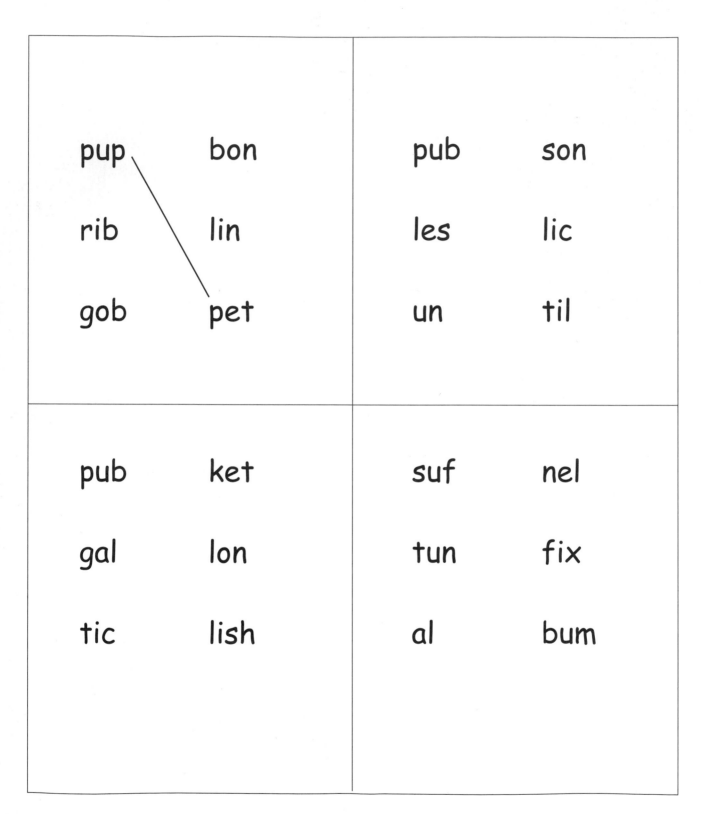

| | | | |
|---|---|---|---|
| pup | bon | pub | son |
| rib | lin | les | lic |
| gob | pet | un | til |
| pub | ket | suf | nel |
| gal | lon | tun | fix |
| tic | lish | al | bum |

Draw a line from a syllable in the first column to a syllable in the second column to create a word.
Read the words.

| | | |
|---|---|---|
| jump | lump | bumper |
| lamp | ramp | jumping |
| camp | limp | limping |
| bump | mumps | damper |
| pump | chimp | camping |
| damp | thump | dumping |
| dump | champ | camper |

help
next

| | |
|---|---|
| ten campers | the next number |
| pumping gas | a damp summer |
| bumped into the desk | on the ramp |
| jumped up | dumped the litter |
| the best helper | next to the lamp |
| under the ladder | after camping |
| the boxing champ | went to help |

Underline and re-read the phrases that tell *where*. Use these phrases in oral sentences.

| | | |
|---|---|---|
| helped | locks | rocking |
| helper | locking | rocks |
| helping | locked | rocked |
| helps | locker | rocker |
| | | |
| asked | kisses | fixing |
| asks | kissing | fixes |
| asking | kissed | fixed |
| | | |
| camps | packed | pitches |
| camped | packs | pitching |
| camper | packing | pitched |
| camping | packer | pitcher |
| | | |
| catches | boxes | matches |
| catcher | boxer | matched |
| catching | boxing | matching |
| | | |
| wishing | singer | telling |
| wishes | singing | tells |
| wished | sings | teller |

| | | |
|---|---|---|
| mixed | packed | punched |
| rushed | licked | dunked |
| lifted | jumped | pumped |
| kissed | handed | limped |
| locked | camped | rented |
| passed | ended | matched |
| hunted | dusted | missed |
| landed | winked | yanked |
| itched | dumped | listed |
| fixed | pitched | bumped |
| wished | hatched | faxed |
| helped | lasted | dented |
| rested | checked | thanked |
| asked | messed | kicked |

Have each student choose a word and use it in an oral sentence.
Circle the words in which the suffix -ed makes the /t/ sound.

1. Mrs. Mills mixed the muffin batter in the pan.

2. My sister just packed her bags.

3. Dan was rushing so he bumped into the ladder.

4. Last summer, some of the kids fished in the pond.

5. Who pinched me?

6. The hens sat on the eggs in the shed and hatched them.

7. The ducks quacked and pecked at the kids!

8. Mrs. Sands asked her husband to put his lunchbox next to the sink.

9. Mr. King wants to put his hammer in the van, but it is locked.

10. Pam missed the bus so she had to run to school.

11. Gus kissed his mom and thanked her for the gift.

12. I wish you had helped me with the dinner dishes.

Underline and re-read the sentences that tell about something that happened that might have been upsetting.